Copyright (c) 2015 by Kimberly Parsons publisher.

All rights reserved. No part of this book may be reproduced by any mechanical, photographic, or electronic process, or in the form of a phonographic recording; nor may it be stored in a retrieval system, transmitted or otherwise be copied for public or private use-other than for "fair use" as brief quotations embodied in articles and reviews-without prior written permission of the publisher.

The author of the book does not dispense medical advise or prescribe the use of any technique as a form of treatment for physical emotional or medical problems without the advice of a physician, either directly or indirectly. The intent of the author is only to offer information of a general nature to help you in your quest for emotional and spiritual well-being. In the event you use any of this information for yourself, which is your constitutional right, the author/publisher assume no responsibility for your actions.

LOVE LIFE

Divine Principles of Love
Messages from God

by
Kimberly Parsons

Introduction

God has given us the Keys to the Kingdom. Love Life will show you how to use those keys to open the doors to your Divine Love Life. Life itself is a miracle and every moment is pure magic that holds infinite possibilities. It is time to awaken to the magnificent angel that you are, a Divine Child of God.

Once you understand the Principles of Divine Love you will be able to open doors you did not even know existed. Love Life shows you how to transform your life from the ordinary to the extraordinary.

Are you ready to awaken to your Higher Self and to the infinite possibilities that await you? I believe that you are, remember there are no mistakes, only wonderful synchronicity's that guide us throughout our Love Life.

About the Author

Kimberly Parsons is a Reiki II practitioner, crystal healer and clairvoyant that works closely with the ascended masters, elemental and the angelic realms. She is the author of Love Life and upcoming children's books. Since childhood she has had an interest in spiritual studies. As a young woman in her early twenties she asked God for answers to help explain the miraculous events that were unfolding in her life. She studied books of great spiritual masters from around the world, but the teachings of Jesus are her favorite. Love Life is a culmination of these spiritual teachings and knowledge she receives in meditation. Her passion for knowledge has brought her to where she is today, a teacher of Divine wisdom.

Gratitude

Thank You God, Divine Source of All for all the Blessings of Love, Support and Divine guidance You give me daily in my magical Blessed Love Life. Thank You and God Bless Your messengers the archangels, ascended masters and my personal guides and angels for all of their Love, support and the Divine Wisdom You so graciously bestow on me. Dear Holy Father/Mother/God I am filled with Love, joy, bliss and eternal gratitude with all the energy of my being, I love You.

Great Love and thanks to Mama, Jenny, Stacy, Dylan, Linda, Jim, the rest of my wonderful family and dearest friends. I picked the best loving hearts to share my Love Life with on this beautiful planet Gaia. Thank you God for loving me through them and loving them through me. For on our own we do nothing, it is Love that loves through us. Namaste.

Table of Contents:

Chapter One: DISCOVERY OF SELF 1

Chapter Two: THE I AM PRESENCE 12

Chapter Three: THE LAW OF ATTRACTION - ASK AND IT IS GIVEN 15

Chapter Four: THE POWER TO CREATE 31

Chapter Five: MEDITATION 36

Chapter Six: TAKING THE JOURNEY – THE EYE OF WISDOM 41

Chapter Seven: ASKING FOR A SIGN 54

Chapter Eight: THE VIOLET FLAME 57

Chapter Nine: DISCOVERING OF SELF —— PART 2 61

Chapter Ten: MUSIC THE LANGUAGE OF LOVE 69

Chapter Eleven: THE POWER OF LOVE 72

Chapter Twelve: FORGIVENESS 75

Chapter Thirteen: MAGNIFICENT BELOVED ANGELS 82

Chapter One

DISCOVERY OF SELF

**ILLUMINATION -
Seek your destiny
and soon discover.
Love, Light,
the Truth you will uncover.**

Good morning dearest sweet angels, time to awaken. You have been having a bad dream. Time to awaken to the beautiful magnificent Divine illuminating angel that is you. Yes!!! YOU!!!

You have been living in the dream, under the veil of illusion for a very long time. So long, that you have come to believe the dream is reality. In case you did not know, the truth is you are a Divine Child of God, God Individualized and it is time to remember and claim your Divine Birthright, which is a Divine Love Life of joy, peace, prosperity and perfect health. God has given you everything you need to create your most magnificent Love Life. Now it is time to learn how to use those gifts.

Conscious Awareness -
The minds consciousness inspire the Eternal Light's fire.

Our Divine Creator, God is pure Love and you are created in God's image so you are also a divine creator of pure Love and you are the creator of your Divine Love Life. You came here to play, to have fun creating new experiences and expand your awareness in the process. The situations and experiences we learn here on Earth is like no other place. We expand our knowledge base for ourselves and for all of life in the Universe. For as we learn and experience in our Love Life, all the other realms benefit from our knowledge as well. Like a drop of water falling into a pond, the ripples effect the entire body of water. We are all One with the Creator Love and everything we experience effects the whole. For everything that we experience, the Oneness of All share in our experiences. One for all for all are One.

Student Teacher -
As I learn I seem to teach
of Love's words I do speak.
As I learn I seen to speak
true Love songs lessons I teach.

The Heavens salute us for being here. This adventure takes great courage and of course pure faith. Our angelic family knows living in the dense third dimension world of Earth is no easy task. As of December 2012 we and the Earth, Gaia have been raised up from a third dimension to the fourth dimension and now we are moving into the the fifth dimension. Our DNA has been upgraded as we prepare for our Ascension.

With so much going on all around us it's no wonder we get bogged down in just the day to day activities, but I wish for everyone to know that we can ask for assistance at any time for we are surrounded by the angelic realms who are here to help us along our path of Ascension. The Creator has decreed our time of freedom has come.

FOREIGN WAYS -
Where am I going? Ways do matter.
Gather your life. Straighten whats scattered.

It is easy to get lost in the illusion, and some may feel there is no way out from where they are. Like being lost in a maze, if one could just raise themselves up, one could easily see the way out, but there is so much weighing one down it seems impossible to get out. There is always a way and once you discover your path you will say, "Wow, now I see, I know which way to go" you will know your True Self, your Life Purpose and you will know your way through this life. No longer will you be effected by the winds of change, but you will take charge of your destiny. You will be the change in your life and successful beyond what you now believe possible.

For those who feel they have lost their way, there are many angels with you this very minute, waiting for you to ask for their help. These heavenly beings all love you very much my beloveds as does God. The moment you ask for God's help then it is done. Throughout the World there are Light workers shining their light brightly, like beacons in the night, we are here to guide you. Call upon the ascended masters Saint Germaine or Jesus, Mother Mary or Moses, Kwan Yin or Buddha, Babaji or Lady Nada, there are many ascended masters too many to mention them all, but know that they are all ready to assist us in our ascension process. Call upon the ones you feel most comfortable with.

As a child I asked my mother what Hell was, she said Hell is the absence of God.

For some people their lives are a living hell, but it does not have to be. Know this, that God is never absent from us, the illusion we live in would make us believe differently, but in reality He is always with us, sometimes it seems like we are alone, but we are not. It is impossible for us to be separate from God.

INTERIOR -
Baby, you are not alone.
Maybe, if you look closer
there is someone home.

TRUTH -
Midst darkness -
I find my destiny.
For the brightest Light,
shines within me.

You Are the Light. Within your heart is where you will find the brightest Light of All, the Shadowless Light of our Father, the Three Fold Flame. The Light of God never fails and this magnificent Light is within you my beloveds. The answers to everything is within your heart center. The brightest Light shines within you, God's Light and you are made of God's Omnipresence Light Substance. We are God Individualized.

Once you discover the Truth and see your True Self, your Higher Self, the illuminating beautiful angelic being that you are, you are free. No longer will you live in fear nor allow fear to rule you. Fear is an illusion (false evidence appearing real), there is only Love, rise up see beyond the illusion.

Valour -
Once I release my fears, my hands are free to grasp Life's meaning.

There are so many things I wish to tell all of my beloved family on this planet. Let me start by saying just how much I love all of you and how proud I am of every soul that volunteered to be here at this time and to shine your benevolence. Honestly, you have no idea what courage it took to come here in this Earth plane at this time and to take part in the great energy work happening in our World now.

Many of you don't even realize just how absolutely wonderful and magnificent you truly are. You are magnificent beings of Divine Light Energy. A Divine child of God. Are you really grasping this statement? Children of God Omnipresence, God Almighty, The I AM Presence. God Individualized, I will keep saying this until it really sinks in. We are all One with God and each other. Everyone you see is an expression of our Creator Love, so create and express Love for everyone you see.

Almighty -
Love is present the Flame I see. So unassuming and always within me.

Being a Divine Child has some really great perks that perhaps many of you might have missed in your Love Life 101 handbook.

Where is your handbook you might ask? Let me remind you, (because believe me you already know all of this, I am helping you to remember) God has equipped us with everything we could ever possibly wish for at any given time in our lives. Think about it, when you plan a vacation or a trip, you plan every detail. How you will get there, where you will stay, what you will do while you are there and what you will take with you for your trip. You leave nothing to chance. So with that being said, do you think your life here is just a chance happening? Not a chance. This has all been carefully planned out by none other than you. No one came to Earth by accident.

When you decided to come to Earth, you planned your life out. You went before the High Council and told them in great detail of your plans and what exactly your goals and desires were and what you would accomplish in this life stream. You mapped it out. You chose the family in which you would be born to help you reach your spiritual goals that you Yourself (your Higher Self) have planned as your Life Purpose.

Our purpose is to have fun, we are playing in this life, it is only when we start taking things seriously that we get into trouble.

Do you remember when you were a child playing outside? Everyday was a new adventure, we could not wait to get outside and play. Before embarking on this journey, while we were still in the Heavenly Realms, we were so excited about coming here like a child waiting to go to Disneyland, everyday would be a new adventure. We would be living on the Edge of Creation shooting forth new ideas and creating and manifesting new wonderful loving fun ways of living. Expanding our consciousness beyond what anyone ever thought possible. Raising our vibration from a third dimension to the fifth dimension or higher while still in our physical bodies. The ascended masters came to show us that ascension in the physical body is possible. Usually one ascends to the higher dimensions in spirit not the physical body like we are doing right now.

We knew before we came that when we arrived here a veil would be drawn over our memory, it is as if we were born with amnesia, we would forget who we truly are, our memory of our Divine Essence would be hidden from us. Like a super hero who has lost their powers. We have not lost our powers, we just forgot we have them. As time went by events would trigger our memories, those Deja vu moments we experience, that make us stop and ask the questions "Who am I?" and "Where did I come from?" "Is this really what my life was meant to be or is there something more" and "there has to be more to life than what was being shown to us?" "What is my purpose here?" We would question our very existence and reason for being here. This would hopefully lead us to the path of Self discovery or Self Realization. There are no mistakes, remember this. It is no mistake that you are reading this book. You have asked and the answers are coming to you. This is such a wonderful time to be here. The Heavens are watching our progress. God has declared our Victory and Freedom. What we are accomplishing here and now has never been done before. Talk about living on the "cutting edge."

In the Etheric Realms we knew coming here would be so fantastic, experiencing life and shooting forth new ideas and creations beyond what has ever been conceived or created before. As we prepared for our time on Earth we were all so excited about our dreams that we wished to fulfill. Going before the High Council and making our case to them about what we plan to accomplish during our time here. The High Council would deliberate our goals and when they could see that it would not only benefit the individual but, would also be for the highest good of all. Then the High Council would allow the individual to come to Earth.

Believe me when I tell you that there are many, many souls that wish to come here at this time. We are the very lucky few that were chosen to come during this magnificent age. This is a great honor for each of us. We are for the first time ever involved in helping an entire planet evolve in consciousness. Not only our own consciousness is expanding and raising up from the third dimension to the fifth and/or higher dimension while in physical form, but an entire planet Earth "Gaia" is raising it's dimensions also. What would normally take hundreds of years and many lifetimes is happening right now in this one lifetime. What we are experiencing can only be accomplished right now. There is no coming back here to try this again to advance our soul hundreds of years, the time is NOW.

I know what you are thinking, how am I going to do this? I don't know what to do, I am challenged just getting to work on time, how will I evolve into the fifth dimension much less help Gaia? Remember that you came here equipped with everything you need for this journey. The time has come for you to remember who you are and where you came from, to awaken to your true identity, your Divine Self. You are so much more than the physical body you see in the mirror, which by the way our physical body is quite amazing, God's creations are Divine.

The Love Life 101 handbook I mentioned earlier, you carry with you all the time. It is your Divine connection with God, the Truth of All That Is. We are Light, Divine

Children of God created in God's Image of Self-Luminous, Intelligent, Omnipotence. Our Electronic Body of Light, The Shadowless Light, The Light of God that never fails and the Mighty I AM Presence is that Light. The Flame of God is within our heart chakra, it is called the Three Fold Flame, that is our Divine spark and connection to our Higher Self and the Creator, the Source of all life. This Divine Spark is a gift from Source and is in the hearts of every son and daughter of God. God is Pure Love and we are created in Love's image. We are His children and we are Divine Magnificent Beings of Love. When we focus our energies on our heart chakra, we are opening ourselves up to Love, we are opening up to God. When we are open and/or seek God's Love and allow Love to flow through our hearts, life will be like the longest lucky streak you have ever had. Everything will go your way. It is amazing, all the blocks or closed doors will suddenly open. You will feel like everyone is rolling out the red carpet for you.

* Matthew 6:33 (KJV) "But seek ye first the Kingdom of God, and His righteousness and all these things shall be added onto you."

For centuries many have allowed the ego full control of their lives consciously or unconsciously, but as we move into the higher dimensions that time is over. Now is the time for new ways of thinking with our hearts and not our minds. When we stop listening to our ego mind chatter telling us we are not good enough, smart enough, rich enough, pretty enough or thin enough, whenever we look at ourselves and find fault, when our minds talk about lack in any way that is fear based illusion, your ego. Do not believe that negative mind chatter, your ego self is constantly trying to feed you. The ego has a purpose, to help protect us, but the ego is overly protective. Part of our journey is to temper the mind with our hearts. The heart is our natural Divine intuition. How many times has our intuition told us to take this pathway, but our minds said to take another pathway. So we believed our mind that at the time seemed more logical, only to discover later that our first intuition was the right path to take. The mind only knows logic, the heart is Divine Wisdom, Power and Love.

Chapter Two

THE I AM PRESENCE

I AM THAT I AM

When we say "I AM," we are actually saying "God in me" and anything you say behind these two words is an extremely powerful manifestation. For example: I AM LOVE, I AM PERFECT HEALTH, I AM ABUNDANCE, I AM JOY, I AM THAT I AM. These are wonderful manifestation affirmations. All of us are one with God. Our "I AM" Presence" aka "Electronic Body" is our Higher Self, God Individualized. As above so below, we are Beings of pure Love, Joy, Omnipotent, Omnipresence. Our Higher Self, our God Self that stays in the Heavenly Realms watching over us and guiding us throughout our life streams. The I AM Presence is God the Father and is composed of God's Sacred Fire which vibrates so rapidly that it remains eternally beautiful, youthful and perfect in all ways. Our Higher Self, the I AM Presence is surrounded by seven concentric spheres of spiritual energy that makes up what is called our "causal body." These spheres of pulsating energy contain the records of all the good works and deeds you have performed since your first incarnation here on earth. It is your treasure-trove in Heaven.

Since we cannot perceive that high dimension of vibration in our physical body a stepped down version of our I AM Presence was created. Without compromising our I AM Presence, this second body is our "Holy Christ Presence" as stated in the Bible "the only begotten of the Father" and remains perfect in all ways no matter what is happening to our physical bodies.

*John 14:6, (KJV) "Jesus saith unto him, I am the way, the truth, and the life: no man cometh unto the Father, BUT BY ME."

To connect with our I AM Presence we must first connect with our Holy Christ Presence. We do this by raising our own vibration to the Higher frequencies through meditation and prayer.

Our physical body is connected to our I AM Presence and our Holy Christ Presence by a cord of light called the Silver Cord or the Crystal Cord. It is this Crystal Cord that connects us with our Higher Self and our Holy Christ Presence. The Crystal Cord is connected to our physical body through our Crown Chakra (seventh chakra at the top of our head) down our spine to our Heart Chakra (fourth chakra at our heart center) where the Divine Spark of God lives in each of us. This Divine Spark is called the "Three Fold Flame," this Holy Trinity is the Sun center and Source of Life to the physical body. The Three Fold Flame is located in a secret compartment in our hearts and stands only 1/16th of an inch, but once you start to fan your Three Fold Flame through meditation and prayer the Three Fold Flame can reach up to an inch in height. The Three Fold Flame is represented by three feather plumes, a pink one for Love, a yellow one for Wisdom and a blue one is for Power.

The Pink plume is for Divine Love, quality of mercy, compassion, justice and creativity.

The Yellow plume is for wisdom, relating to illumination, the right use of knowledge, the expansion of intelligence of the Godhead into the chalice of the heart and mind.

The Blue plume is for spiritual power, relates to faith, goodwill and the Divine intent.

When you meditate, enter the silence and connect with your Higher Self, your God Self you are connecting with your I AM Presence.

Chapter Three

THE LAW OF ATTRACTION - ASK AND IT IS GIVEN

- *** Matthew 7:7 - Luke 11:9 Ask, and it shall be given you; seek, and ye shall find; knock, and it shall be opened unto you.**

- *** Matthew 21:21-22 Verily I say unto you, If ye have faith, and doubt not, ye shall not only do this which is done to the fig tree, but also if ye shall say unto this mountain, be thou removed, and be thou cast into the sea; it shall be done.**

- *** And all things, whatsoever ye shall ask in prayer, believing, ye shall receive.**

- *** Mark 11:24 Therefore I say unto you, What things soever ye desire, when ye pray, believe that ye receive [them], and ye shall have them.**
  (* The New Testament, King James Version)

Anything your heart desires you may have. This is why it is so important to keep our thoughts on the highest most positive levels for the best possible outcomes of our desires and wishes. We are divine creators if you realize that or not, it is true. What are you thinking about? Whatever it is that is what you are creating. If you are happily moving through your world then you are creating more things to be happy about. If you are worrying, then you are creating more things to worry about.

These are very powerful positive affirmations. When you say the words "I AM" anything you say after these words you will manifest.

I AM Love
I AM Joy
I AM Perfect Health
I AM Abundance
I AM Youth and Beauty
I AM Bliss
I AM Magnificent
I AM Truth
I AM the Eternal, Transcendent, Electronic Body of Ascended Master Light
I AM Prosperity
I AM the Ascension in the Light
I AM THAT I AM
I AM I AM I AM ONE with the Holy Christ Consciousness
I AM an Ultimate Divine Receiver of the Bliss, Abundance, Truth, and Love of the Creator.

We truly are such magnificent beings of Divine Love Light, so much more than we can even fathom with our human minds. You can truly create the most fantastic life you ever believed possible. Everything is what you believe, your thoughts are the things that you are creating.

Love life

Jesus told us that with faith everything is possible as long as one believes.

Be happy, be excited and know without a doubt that you have created all of your dearest wishes and dreams right now. God has infinite abundance so there is no limit to how much abundance each one of us can manifest in our life. Do not settle for a mediocre life when you can create a magnificent life and fulfill your life purpose. Remember the more abundance you create the more you are able to share with others. Whatever a person dreams of can be manifested. Start taking actions to build your ideal life. Sit down with pen and paper and outline what it is exactly you wish to create. Writing down your dreams and goals will help you to manifest them faster. "I am so happy and grateful now that (fill in your dreams here)." Cut a picture out of a magazine or print a picture from your computer of what you wish to achieve in your life and put it on your vision board. This technique is called creative visualization and helps you to consciously create exactly what you wish for using the Law of Attraction. Just ten minutes a day visualize your life the way you wish it to be. I do manifestation and visualizations while driving to places. Turn off the radio and turn on the manifestation energy. Tell God exactly what you require and thank Him for always answering your prayers immediately. It is done. What have you always wanted to do in your life? I am not asking how do you make your living now but, what is your dream career or business? What are you passionate about? Whatever your dream is you can manifest that dream into reality.

Start taking baby steps daily to manifesting your dreams. Once you allow yourself to express your true talents your life will change for the better in all ways. Love all aspects of your life now. What ever you wish to create in your life ask God for assistance in manifesting your dreams. All of Heaven will work with you to accomplish your goals. You are never alone. Once you ask God there is no need to keep asking, you only have to ask once. When you order something online you only place your order once and you know it is going to come, you do not keep ordering it over and over. The same is true with asking God for anything in your life. Once you ask, now you envision yourself as already having it. See yourself happily driving your new car, living in your dream home, working in your desired career or business or happily walking hand in hand on the beach with your Twin Flame. Thank God for making all your dreams a reality. Joy, faith and trust are the keys that unlock the doors to Heavenly Abundance.

Now that you have asked God for His assistance pay attention to any ideas or inspirational thoughts that come to mind and take action, for they will lead you where you need to go. It may not seem apparent at first, but God always has a wonderful plan custom made for each of us. Have faith in yourself and the ideas that come to you for they are Divinely inspired. Remember how magnificent you are, a shining star my beloved brothers and sisters. Abundance and wealth are your natural birth right and you are worthy to receive your blessings now. Let go of any negative thoughts or feelings and allow the flow of abundance into your life.

Richard Branson and Bill Gates are two perfect examples of very successful entrepreneurs, do you think when they start a business they are wondering if it will fail? Failure is not in their vocabulary it does not exist for them. What these two men have in common is that they are not afraid to try something new. If you stumble and fall get back up and keep going, do not give up.

You must believe in God and yourself. See your life as being the success you wish it to be now. Believe and achieve. Envision your life in full color and glory, smile and love everything you have created and be filled with joy and gratitude that all of your dreams have become reality. And so it is.

I AM an Ultimate Divine Receiver of the Bliss, Abundance, Truth, and Love of the Creator.

I once received a text, no name on it, just this message which I love, "Beauty has no weight limit." That is so true. Many women belittle themselves daily finding fault with some part of their body. God tells us that we are perfect just the way we are. We are beautiful magnificent beings and we need to recognize this in ourselves right this very minute. No more negative mind chatter. If you could just quiet that incessant chatter and truly listen to your heart that speaks so softly, so lovingly, then you truly are listening to God speaking to you. God will always send you calm uplifting messages of Love. He will lift your spirit to new heights, make you feel great about yourself, encourage you to follow your hearts desire and to be the absolute best in this life. God sees the beauty in all of us and wishes for you to see it in yourselves also. He wishes to help you with everything in your life, but you must ask for His help. God gave us Free Will, part of His Universal Laws. Free Will is a wonderful gift, which means He allows us to live our lives the way we wish to. If you wish for God's help you must ask for it. God's help is always freely given to all that ask. Ask and you shall receive.

I have always been so independent, strong willed, and determined to do everything myself that I seldom would think to ask for help. A few years ago I was applying for a loan to do some repairs and remodeling to my house and to pay off some debts. I knew the bank would lend me the money for the repairs and remodel but I was not sure about getting the money to pay off the debts. I was pondering in my mind would the bank allow me to do this or would the loan only cover the repairs. I prayed to God for guidance and help. A couple of days later I received a call from the bank. The manager's voice was hesitant, I could tell there was something she was holding back about the loan. She asked me if I could come in so we could discuss the matter. I said sure, but what is it. I could not wait until that afternoon to know what she wished to talk to me about. She said I could get the loan I asked for but with some of the money I would have to pay off my debts and what was left I could use to do repairs and remodel my house. I was thrilled to hear this news. This is exactly what I wanted to do, but the bank manager did not know this and thought I would be upset over her news. Here was the answer to my prayers. "Thank you God!!!" I exclaimed after hanging up the phone. I immediately put my hands together and sent prayers of gratitude to God. God is always answering our prayers.

Another example came one chilly fall day when I was trying to close the double gates in my backyard fence. There are two iron bolts that fasten the gates completely. The first bolt closed easily but, the second iron bolt I was having difficulty getting it to close. The gate had to be bolted no doubt about that. Winter was coming and if the gate was not securely fastened the weight of the snow piled on it from the local snow plow on this gateway would press so hard it would break the gate. So I was pushing with all my body against the gates and the second bolt was so close, just centimeters away from closing but it would not close. It was fall in Wisconsin and it was a very cold day and the wind was blowing hard. In other words, it was bitter cold outside. I had been trying to lock this gate for more than thirty minutes, but it would not budge. I was freezing cold, FINALLY with tears of frustration running down my face, I asked God for help. "God, if you would please help me lock this gate I promise I will never unlock it again!" The very instant I asked for help the iron bolt immediately slammed closed. Immediately!!!! "Thank you God!!!" I exclaimed. I have kept my promise to God, I have not opened that gate again.

When I finally smartened up and decided to ask for help, WOW!!!! GOD DELIVERS!!!! ASK AND YOU SHALL RECEIVE!! Without exception.

God is the best life coach I could ever hope for. He helps me with everything. There is nothing too small to ask for guidance, and why not, God knows exactly what is best for us at any given time.

I have to mention this event since my whole family was a witness to this miracle. One day back in Dallas, Texas my mother, sister Jenny and I were all home sick with a cold. It was a cold rainy day and as we were bundled up in blankets on the couch trying to sooth our colds we wished we had some firewood, how cozy we would be to have a warm fire in the fireplace. "God I wish we had some firewood." I said. We all envisioned this wonderful fire but with everyone in the house sick, no one was going to go to the store to buy any. A few minutes later there was a knock at our door. When we opened the door the man standing there asked us if we would like to buy some firewood. "Yes, please" we said. As the man was stacking up the firewood, we all just looked at each other and smiled. This was a blessing from God no doubt. Instant manifestation. God had firewood delivered to our home, He granted our wish. We were all very happy and cozy with our box of tissues and a cup hot tea sitting in

Love life

front of a warm fire. What a wonderful blessing. Thank you God.

God is here for all things in our lives, we just have to allow Him in. God loves to be a part of our day to day lives. He loves us unconditionally and of course He wishes the best life possible for His children. Some might think it is a sign of weakness to ask for God's help, when in reality it is just the opposite. I would tell myself "Aw, God is much too busy with more important things than to be bothered with this, I can handle this myself." I always thought He was too busy for the little things in my life, but that is the farthest thing from the truth, nothing is too small or trivial for His help. God has an entire team of Heavenly Angels, Archangels, and Ascended Masters ready and willing to help us at any time. Everyone has an entire Heavenly staff of Coworkers ready to jump in and help us, all we have to do is ask them nicely and help is given. ASK AND IT IS ALWAYS GIVEN. I talk to God daily, if nothing else to thank Him for all my blessings He has bestowed on me. Then I will start naming my blessings so He knows I really do appreciate His gifts of Love. It is important to be grateful be thankful for all that you have.

Every time you ask for something God always gives it to you. Now I know what you are thinking, I have asked God and asked God, but God never answers "I never get what I want!". I am saying Yes, God does answer, I promise you God always answers. It is only one's lack of faith that brings the undesired outcome. Many times just before your request arrives you give up, you lose faith and say, "I knew it was too good to be true, God never answers my prayers." Ok, God will now give you exactly what you just asked for, disappointment and lack. It is imperative that you keep your faith strong, your thoughts and visions must be on the positive outcome that you wish. Envision your desires as though they are already manifested in all areas of your life, your career or business, your lifestyle, your personal relationships and your health, because you are manifesting your future right now with your thoughts.

Here is a KEY to getting what you ask for "COMPLETE FAITH." BELIEVE AND ACHIEVE. Do you remember what faith is? Faith is believing in something without having proof. You will need unwavering faith to make your dreams a reality. Faith and trust, EXPECT to see God make your dreams a reality, expect miracles to manifest now. If you wish to see miracles in you life you first must BELIEVE in miracles. So many times people ask God for something they truly want and in the beginning they are really excited about it, and the Universe is creating their desires. It is important to "allow" God to manifest your dreams and desires into reality. This could happen instantly or it can take some time, we must be patient and trust, trust, trust and keep the faith. As time goes by people lose faith and say, "My dreams never come true." Well, the Universe will create that wish for you also. People tend to give up just before their dreams are manifested into this reality. In many cases the wished for dreams are in the final stages ready for manifestation, but people loose faith in the eleventh hour, stating their dreams never come true so their wishes are granted for that as well. What a shame. Keep the faith and trust strong, then watch your dreams become reality. With God all things are possible.

*Mark 9:23 (KJV) Jesus said, "If thou canst believe, all things are possible to those that believe." Jesus is saying, if you can believe then all things are possible.

Ok, is that sinking in? Not some things or a few things, but ALL THINGS ARE POSSIBLE IF A PERSON BELIEVES. GOD IS ALL THINGS, GOD HAS NO LIMITATIONS~!!!! Amen to that.

What ever we are thinking about we are creating. Thoughts are things, thoughts are energy, we are pure energy and our emotions are indicators of what we are creating. If we are feeling good then our thoughts are creating what we wish to create, if our thoughts do not feel good, then we are creating more of what we do not want. Think of it this way, you are the captain of your ship and your thoughts are on the wheel steering the your life ship. Where is your life heading? Take control of your thoughts and steer your life in the direction you wish to go.

If you do not like what you see, you can change your direction by simply changing your mind, be a conscious creator. When you choose better feeling thoughts, your life will change for the better. It really is that simple. I know what you are thinking. How do I control my thoughts? Like trying anything new we have to practice new ways of doing things. For some it may take longer to erase the old conditioning and incorporate these new ideas and ways of thinking and living our lives while others may make the changes quickly and easily. Once you start, you will notice immediately how good you feel. Keeping your thoughts, words and actions more positive has immediate benefits. Keep your conversations impeccable. There is an old saying, "If you don't have anything nice to say then say nothing at all." If you keep your thoughts on the highest possible level you will feel great and when you are feeling great you attract more of the things you wish to have in your life. The possibilities are limitless.

Follow your hearts desires, if that is being an artist, musician, world leader, inventor, chef, baker, engineer, healer or teacher what ever your special gift is do what makes you happy. When you are doing what makes you happy, then you are being of service to God, service to the Light, because you are fulfilling your Life Purpose. Everyone has a special unique gift to offer our world. It is very important for everyone to fulfill their life purpose whatever that maybe. The great news is that our life purpose is always something that we love to do. It is our hearts desire. When our work is our hearts desire, then it no longer feels like work, but it is exhilarating and time passes quickly, before we know it our work day is done and it is time for fun.

Love life

A few years ago, I was looking around at our world and asking God how will we turn this around. The entire world seem to be in a tail spin and I was asking how will we be able pull up out of this. Everyone is so busy just trying to keep their heads above water, how can we pull together to create a better world for everyone, not just the one percent. I could see that we really need a whole new way of living, thinking and governance, to live on Gaia and respect and love her and all the other life forms here. Gaia has the right to live as she was intended. Gaia is the most beautiful mother to many beings and we must respect all of her children. No longer can we act like spoiled children on the playground. We must clean up after ourselves and be loving to all of Gaia's children. We have been given a most magnificent blessed gift of life on Gaia. Imagine how much farther along we would be as a civilization had we just used our resources for the betterment of all, instead of wasting them in wars. Billions of dollars spent on military programs that in the end killed people, destroyed cities and nature. Then after the wars the cities had to be rebuilt which in turn more resources are used. When we could have used those funds for natural sources of free energy, education, agriculture, transforming and building green cities and urban areas. The time of wars is over, it is time for renewal, growth, education and most of all LOVE. "There is nothing to fear but fear itself." Franklin D. Roosevelt. Fear (false evidence appearing real) is the illusion, there is only Love.

Everyone on this planet is God individualized and we are all one with God and each other. This Oneness we all share is a Sacred Divine Energy that connects us to everyone and every thing. Everything is alive with energy. This Divine Energy is found even in the trees, grass, rocks and stones, everything. I can imagine what must be going through some of your minds, "no way am I connected with everyone on this planet." Let me assure you my brothers and sisters truly you are.

Comments -
World of mirrors reflect on me, things that should or should not be.

We are like mirrors reflecting images back to each other. Sometime we love what is reflected in the mirrors and they bring us great joy and love and sometimes we do not. What we dislike in others is a mere reflection of what we dislike in ourselves though this may not always be apparent to us. If you dislike characteristics you see in someone, then you are being offered a gift, an opportunity for you to examine your own thoughts or ideals. Sometimes the mirror is difficult to look at, but if we are truthful with ourselves we can adjust our thoughts from the old way we were conditioned to think to a more Divinely inspired way of thinking and looking at our world. This is another example of like attracts like. So if we do not like what we see in the mirror all we have to do is change our thoughts to attract what we do like.

QUEST FOR LIFE -
Who made the plans?
Who wrote the book?
So many demands.
No time to look.

Running all day
and into night.
Who is to say
wrong from right?

I want to know
the knowledge I seek.
For pretty or show,
wild or meek.

Who wrote the rules?
Time to revise.
Build with new tools.
Time for the wise!

There must be more like I,
who speak the Truth?
To correct this bad score.
What happened to couth?

What could be right,
in evil men.
Forging ruthless spite,
devastating sin.

Kimberly Parsons

**Minds slammed closed,
no entrance to be found.
Asleep or just dosed,
blocking out sound.**

**Long is my quest,
for someone to hear.
How can they jest,
about unspeakable fear.**

**Will anyone listen,
before it's too late.
Children's eyes now glisten,
soon a teary state.**

**We have the power
to change our fate.
For God gave us
the power to Create.**

Chapter Four

THE POWER TO CREATE

At the time I wrote Quest for Life, I did not realize the full potential of the words "The power to Create." Of course I knew we create things, just look at our world and you will see man made creations are everywhere. All of these creations were at one point someones thoughts. For many people do not yet realize that everything in our own personal world we have created, whether we consider them good or bad, like it or not it is true. Many still do not understand that thoughts are things. Everything is Energy, our thoughts are energy and we must now be "Conscious creators." So that each one of us will create only the things we wish to have in our lives. I am an artist, photographer and writer and I create all the time. It was not until I "awakened' that I discovered just how magnificent God created us. We are His children made by Him in His image. Most people think his image is like our physical body but it is not, His image is like the Pure Light of a Thousand Suns shining in such Dazzling Splendor, Power and Perfection.

Like our Father/Mother/God we can create anything we wish to. ANYTHING! Now we're talking. Anything I desire or wish for I can create including a better life for myself and the world. We can create anything we wish including a better world for all of us to live in now, we can even create planets, stars and entire galaxies if we so desire. We are creating all the time. Thoughts are things. Everything is energy including us and where we place our energy (our thoughts) is what we shall create. What do you think about? Are you imagining a world of Divine perfection, Gaia clean and restored to the garden of Eden, a peaceful world of abundance with plenty of food, clothing and beautiful places to call home for everyone. Let us remove the word shelter from our vocabulary. Shelters bring up visions of lack. Instead lets start using words like great abundance and beautiful homes, magnificent dwellings for all of our brothers and sisters. I hear laughter of complete joy coming from everyone on Gaia. This is truly a magnificent gift, the gift of creation.

Conscious Levels - Poor is only a state of mind.

Are you visualizing your life as the dream come true, living in the home of your dreams, traveling the world, creating your own successful business, or are you worrying about your future, how will you pay the bills, feed the family, find a better job or find a job, lose weight, or get healthy? Your thoughts are creating your future right now. So if you are worrying then you are creating the very thing you are worrying about, but if you are happily seeing yourself living the abundant, happy, loving, healthy joyful lifestyle of your dreams then you are creating that. It is important for you to keep your thoughts happy, highly positive and on the desired results, see it as if you have already manifested your highest goals and dreams now and so it is.

* **Mark 11:24 (KJV) Therefore I say unto you, What things so ever ye desire, when ye pray, believe that ye receive [them], and ye shall have them.**

When visualizing do not think soon or someday, because soon or someday never arrives because it will always be in the future. If something is "on it's way" or "coming" it will always be on its way, it will never arrive because it is a future event. Imagine, focus on your desires, visualize you are living the dream "NOW." Now is all there is, "RIGHT NOW." This is what Jesus is telling us when Jesus said, "believe that ye receive them."

You know how to day dream, to visualize is the same as daydreams, so get busy, day dream away my friends in your dream home, in a peaceful world, unlimited prosperity, blissfully happy in a relationship, living the life you are meant to live, a beautiful healthy body, and love every detail that you see. Be excited about your wonderful life and express your joy and gratitude to God, tell Him just how happy and thrilled you are to be living your dream NOW. Instead of working so hard to make it happen all by yourself, ask God and then go with the Divine flow. Follow those intuitive thoughts and allow the flow of abundance to come to you. Express gratitude for all your blessings that you already have right now will speed up the process and God will send you immediate blessings right back. Heaven loves to hear prayers of gratitude and will immediately send you more things to be grateful for.

POSITIVE POWER
Everyday I make my dreams come true, success of mind will work for you.

Here are three simple steps to creating your best Love Life.

1. Imagine
2. Communicate
3. Expect

1. First image what it is you want to have or experience. Focus clearly on your desired outcome and see yourself as already having it, living your dream now, what ever that dream maybe. Envision yourself in the very situation you desire. You are living the dream now. Be grateful for all the gifts God has bestowed on you. The fastest way to manifest more good things into your life is to give thanks for all that you have or wish to have. I give thanks for the dreams I wish to manifest, see yourself as already having what you wish for. Gratitude speeds up the manifestation process. "Attitude of Gratitude" and "Be Happy!"

2. Communicate your ideas to God. You are a Divine Child of God and anything you desire you can manifest. He showers His children with all that they desire. Tell God exactly what you would like to have or experience. I have a box that I use to put all of my wishes in I call this my " And So It Is" box and every time I think of something I wish to create in my life I

write it down on a piece of paper or print the picture from my computer and I put that picture in the box and as I drop my wished for dream into the box I say, "And So It Is". Focus all of your energies on creating your highest most positive visions. See yourself living your dream. If you can envision it you can create it.

3. Expect what you wish for to manifest in your life. Be confident about your desires and have complete faith that God will bring you all that you desire. Expect miracles and you will see miracles. You must remember to embrace complete faith. Heaven is busy at work creating your dreams come true, don't give up two minutes before they manifest into reality. Keep the Faith!!!

Chapter Five

MEDITATION

VISIONARY HALLS -
Down visionary halls I journey.
Not far from home, only light years away.
Is where I find You, for a short stay.
Reflective consciousness opening doors in this chalet.
Visionary courtyards sends my soul to play.

The world we live in, this illusion we call life, likes to keep us very busy, so busy there is no time to explore our true Selves. Because when you do discover Self, you are free, you are forever FREE. There are many things to distract us in this life, the TV, radio, electronic games, our cell phones. We often feel we do not have enough time in the day to meditate with all that life demands from us. This leaves us feeling stressed, tired, impatient and unhappy.

If you will allow just 10 to15 minutes a day to sit in silence you will find that meditation reduces stress in your daily life. There are so many benefits that come with meditation, finding inner peace is one, transform negative energy to positive, and many health benefits also. Meditation instills calmness to our being, we are more relaxed and better able to handle our daily lives. You will discover how much happier you will become. Cultivating a positive mind set will allow miracles to manifest in your daily life. Meditation is beneficial for everyone. Some of the best benefits of meditation are enlightenment, peace and tranquility, wisdom, joy, happiness, love, compassion, stress reduction, improved brain function, discovering your purpose, gifts, yogic and psychic power, and your Divine Magnificence. Meditation is an important factor in our daily lives. As I started devoting more time to meditation I noticed everything in my life seemed to flow smoothly, because I was more balanced within myself I was sending out a more positive vibration to the world and in turn the world was sending back a more positive vibration to me. You see Law of Attraction is in every facet of our lives. Like attracts like. This is why I talk about the Law of Attraction throughout my book. Our world is a reflection of ourselves, in order for us to better our world we must start by improving ourselves first. Meditation helps bring out the best in us. Once you discover your True Self through meditation, all of your doubts will disappear and your questions will be answered. The Truth will be revealed to you. You will lift the veils of illusion and you will "LOVE" what you discover about your Self. The ancient Greek aphorism "Know Thyself" was inscribed over the temple of Apollo in Delphi. It is one of the of the Delphic Maxims. The greatest ancient Greek philosophers from Plato to Socrates have many different meanings to the phrase "Know Thyself," but most of them agree that people sound ridiculous when trying to figure out hidden mysteries when they have not explored the mystery of themselves first. How can you truly know anything when you do not know who you are? I agree with the Greek philosophers.

Discover your "Self" first, then everything else will fall into place. The world is changing for the better in all ways and so can you. You only need to send out your heartfelt intent to connect with your Higher Self. For example: sit in a quiet place and meditate on these words, **"I require to connect with my Holy Christ Consciousness, my I AM Presence now."** See for yourSelf. Fly high in the direction of your dreams. You will exceed your own expectations, I promise. Don't believe anyone that says you are crazy for believing in your dreams. You are not. We all have different dreams and desires, Thank God! We are all unique, there are no two things exactly alike in all the world, God made us that way, perfect in every aspect. It is our creative differences that make us special and all of life should be honored for the unique gifts we bring. No one else brings the unique gifts that you offer the world. ALL LIFE PATHS are uniquely sacred and worthy of respect.

BURGEON -
I surprisingly uncovered knowledge left unsaid.
Wisdom I discovered cultivating my flower bed.

Daily meditations (preferably the same time each day) play an important role in your spiritual growth. You will notice over time the more you practice meditation the easier it is for you to go into your meditative state. My advice would be to make this one of your top priorities for your own peace of mind. With all that you do for so many others in your life, do this one thing for yourself. One of the best places to meditate is outside, connecting with nature always restores our soul. Sit down right on mother Gaia take off your shoes and wiggle your toes in the grass and allow your energy to merge with hers. Really get connected and send love straight from your heart center to hers. I promise you will feel her sending love right back to you. If you cannot find a quiet place outside, then, by all means, meditate indoors. All that is really important here is to mediate any way or where you can find a quiet place. I find that holding my quartz crystals or stones increases the energy flow. Remember when shopping for crystals or stones follow your intuition, pick the ones you are drawn to, hold them for a few minutes to see if they resonate with you. Don't worry yourself about picking the right stones for you will be drawn to the stones meant for you. Trust your intuition in all that you do, it is your personal guidance system. Crystals and stones are only a suggestion, they are not necessary for you to connect with your Higher Self. You were born with everything you require in this life. Meditation, entering the silence is a key to open the doors in the Heavenly Kingdom. Seek and you will discover.

If you take the time to meditate even for just a few moments to enter the silence each day, your life will change for the better in all areas. It really is time to find a quiet place in our daily lives with no distractions so that we can connect with our Higher Self. The importance of meditation and connecting with our Divine Self is vital in all areas of our lives, especially for our four lower bodies the physical, mental, emotional and spiritual. The answers to all the questions you are seeking are found within your Self.

Talking with God can be done any time any place, not just during meditation. Someone once asked "what is the difference between prayer and meditation?" The difference is in prayer you are talking to God, in meditation you are listening to God. I have learned that I hear God all the time, not just in meditation. I know everyone else can also. You have been hearing Him all along, you just don't believe that was really God's voice because God's voice sounds like our own voice and you thought it was just your thoughts.

THE GUIDE
Open your heart and unlock your mind. The light in your soul is the loving kind.

Chapter Six

TAKING THE JOURNEY – THE EYE OF WISDOM

EYE OF WISDOM -
See the fire
of the eye.
A view of my soul
I cannot hide.
Windows of truth
That bares no lie.
To carry me through
To the other side.

The journey within is very easily done. You are all that you need to take this wonderful journey of Self discovery. There is a little preparation before you meditate, and I do mean very little.

Opening your heart center and allowing the Love Light to flow freely, your spirit is Ascending to the Higher Vibratory Planes of existence and connecting with our Creator.

*Psalms 46:10 (KJV) "BE STILL AND KNOW THAT I AM GOD". For centuries great masters have passed down these sacred teachings all around the world.

The importance of Self Discovery, meditation, taking the journey within. Many are called but few answer. Will you answer the call? Find a quiet place to meditate and tell others that live in your home that you do not wish to be disturbed for the next half hour or so, how ever long your planned meditation will last. I light candles, either white or ivory in color, I love vanilla candles with Nag Champa incense. Candles and incense are not required, but I believe they are beneficial in many ways. They have been used in healing rituals for centuries. The light of candles raises our vibratory field giving us a feeling peace and a sense of calmness, while incense purifies the air and offers a tranquillity effect to the senses. They also dissipate negative energies and create a positive state of mind. Years ago I was taught the Flame meditation, where I would meditate by staring directly into the flame of a candle for long periods of time. The Flame meditation is wonderful to do. You decide for yourself what feels best for you. If you can it is a good idea to meditate at the same time each day if possible, as your body will get use to the schedule and you will be able to move into your quiet meditational state much easier. Next you will want to wear comfortable clothing, and find a comfortable place to sit, either in a comfy armchair with your back straight and your feet flat on the floor or sitting cross legged on a pillow on the floor, or propped up on your bed, whatever you prefer, there is no right or wrong way. Sometimes I sit in the green grass by a river or creek, or on the beach early in the morning before beach goers arrive. The point is to be comfortable, so find a comfortable place to sit. It is best not to lay down because it is too easy to fall asleep. Trust me I know about the falling asleep part first hand. There have been many times even sitting straight up in a chair, that after a meditation I find myself slumped over. I still have the wonderful benefits of meditation. If you fall asleep that is okay. With practice you will improve.

In 2012 we have gone through a major shift in consciousness and now all that is needed to connect to the Higher Realms is to put out our intent. "I now intend to connect with my Holy Christ Consciousness, my Higher Self." This is how easily it is done now. I learned to meditate over thirty years ago, so I included the way in which I learned also. You can choose what works best for you.

The next step is breath exercises. Inhale through your nose very slowly and deeply to the count of eight and now exhale very slowly to the count of eight. Do this exercise five times then allow your breath to breathe on it's own, no controlling the breath. These are big deep breathes and your abdomen and ribs should expand quite a bit as you breathe in. Breath control is one step to help you to reach a higher state of consciousness. Yogi's train their breath so that they breathe in Light and breathe out Love.

The next step will be to relax your entire body. Starting with your feet mentally say "My feet, toes and ankles are completely relaxed, my calves, shins and knees are completely relaxed, my upper legs and thighs are completely relaxed, my hips and buttocks are now completely relaxed, my abdomen and back are completely relaxed, my chest is completely relaxed, my hands, arms and shoulders are completely relaxed, my face and head are completely relaxed." When you relax your face your mouth should open slightly. Now that you are completely relaxed you are ready for the next step of your journey, it is time to go within.

We want to fill our body with Divine golden white Light. We start by envisioning a tube that runs through your Crown chakra (the top of your head) down through your spine (your main chakra system) and out at the your root chakra (at the base of your spine). Envision Divine golden white Light pouring into your Crown Chakra and into this tube filling up your entire body and your Heart Center until your body is filled to overflowing and the Light surrounds the physical body in an orb of Divine Golden White Light. Envision yourself completely immersed in this beautiful orb of Golden White Light.

CONSCIOUS AWARENESS -
The minds consciousness inspire, the Eternal Lights Fire.

With eyes closed put your full attention to your Sixth Chakra, the space just between your eye brows. This area is called your Third Eye, or the Eye of Wisdom and this Chakra is connected to your Pineal Gland. Through the Third Eye and the Pineal gland you will connect with your Holy Christ Presence, the I AM Presence and the

Angelic and Cosmic Realms. We can reach the Higher dimensions, while still remaining in our physical body. This is a gift from God, "Source." Edgar Cayce referred to the pineal gland as the "Seat of the Soul." The pineal gland is in the shape of a small pine cone (hence the name) and it is located near the center of the brain, between the two hemispheres, tucked in a groove where the two rounded thalamic bodies join.

Once the Pineal Gland is activated one can easily access the Higher spiritual realms. Experiencing these Higher vibrations you have a sense of oneness with all the world, the greatest joy and love "nirvana" that you have ever experienced in this lifestream.

The third eye is your connection, your portal to reaching the Highest realms where your Higher Self lives with Source. This is our wonderful gift from God. Throughout history the Pineal Gland can be seen in many cultures and countries, in Rome at the Vatican is where the largest sculpture of a pine cone can be found. The huge statue known as the Pigna (pine) or the Fontana Della Pigna depicts a giant pine cone that many believe represent the Pineal Gland. Also at the Vatican are pine cone candle holders that represent the Eternal Light of God.

In Egypt, the Staff of Osiris, shows two serpents intertwining, rising up to the pine cone at the top of the staff. It is believed by some that the staff is symbolic of the Indian sacred teachings of the "Kundalini" which is the spiritual energy in the body that runs up the spinal column, and connects the Seven Main Chakras, from the root chakra (at the base of the spine) to the crown chakra (the top of the head). When one consciously moves the energy from the Root Chakra up through all seven Chakras to the Crown Chakra Enlightenment occurs in the individual, Awakening occurs. The alignment of the Chakras is said to be the one and only way to attain "Divine Wisdom" which bestows Pure Love, Joy and Divine Knowledge.

*Genesis 32:30 (KJV) Jacob called the name of the place Peniel: "For I have seen God face to face, and my life is preserved. And as he passed over Peniel the sun rose upon him."

The literal Biblical translation of the word "Peniel" means "Face of God".

*Matthew 6:22 (KJV) "The light of the body is the eye: if therefore your eye be single, your whole body shall be full of light."

The Romans and the Egyptian's knew the benefits of the Pineal Gland and one can see in their art works depicting the Pineal Gland with a symbol of an eye. The Eye of Horus in Egypt and the Pineal Gland show striking resemblances. The Assyrian's Deities are shown in ancient carvings with pine cones in their hands. These are just a few of the examples of the importance of the Pineal Gland. Are you ready to look through thy single eye, through the eye of Love?

The Third Eye is a bridge from the physical realm to the Highest spiritual realms. When you first start to meditate you may only see darkness, but wait, give this a little time. It is like being outside on a bright sunny day and then walking inside into a dark room, your eyes need time to adjust to the light. There are endless possibilities of what miracles you will see, so I will only tell you some of the things I have seen and experienced. Beautiful Beings of Light, Angels, Beings from the Elemental realms, the Cosmic realms, and most important my Holy Christ Consciousness and my I AM Presence. Every time I meditate I see new and wonderful sites to behold. I wish you the most wonderful magical journey of Love.

Om or Aum is a mystic syllable and considered the most sacred mantra in the Hindu Sanskrit. In Hinduism it represents omnipotent, omnipresent and the Source of all manifest existence. OM is the vibration of God. When you say "OM" you are saying God and the vibration of this word clears all space, including your mind chatter and connects you with Omnipresence. This is why people from around the world say the word OM when they meditate. You are calling God and clearing the space for you to connect, which is the purpose of meditation. The chanting of OM drives away all worldly thoughts and removes distraction. The sound also resonates and rejuvenates the body. It is sacred. You may chant the word OM if you wish but it is not required to connect with the Creator. The chanting of the word OM does help one stay focused and helps to stop the mind chatter. You decide what works best for you. I sometimes start by saying OM, then remain quiet for the rest of my meditation. It really is up to each individual. I wanted to give a little background information to the sacred word OM, AUM.

As you look through your Third Eye you will start to see movement as different images appear. You always want your intentions be known. You can say "My intent is to connect with Jesus or my Holy Christ Consciousness" or "my I AM Presence," "God," or "only the Highest Beings of the Light." Believe me you will know Jesus and God when you see them. No doubt about it. If anyone appears to you that you have an odd feeling about, ask them if they are of the Light? They cannot say they are if they are not of the Light. If they are not of the Light then ask them to leave now. As many images go by and they are quite amazing, expressing your intentions will help you to stay focused on your purpose and get your where you want to be faster. This also allows the Universe to help you achieve what you wish to achieve from your meditation, you have now made your intensions clear. As you express your desires to Source, Source is eager to manifest them for you.

You may see a spiral of lights, perhaps it looks like stars spiraling. Follow that flow if it resonates with you, see yourself walking or floating up into the spiral. Once in the spiral you may notice one star brighter than all the rest and it seems to dance in front of you. I call that the Angel Light or Angel Star. The Angel Star is your Angel

Guide. Relax and know that everything is flowing as it should and unfolding in Divine Order. Everyone's experience is different, so you might experience a completely different vision. I am just relating one of my meditations. Some people see themselves being guided by angelic beings and getting on an elevator and going up and when the door opens they are standing in the presence of their Holy Christ Presence. There are as many paths to your Higher Self as there are souls. Each path is uniquely different. Love Life because it is a fantastic ride. When you reach the Door of Light, Heaven's Door, step into this Light now. When I was standing at the doorway I heard a voice say, "Hurry, there's not much time!" Then I saw my grandmother standing in the door of Light and I stepped into the Light, Heaven Divine. I wrote about my meditation and connecting with my Higher Self, but honestly words cannot express the great Love and Bliss I felt standing in the Presence of Jesus, my I AM Presence and the angelic realm. To experience the connection with our Holy Christ Presence and our I AM Presence is our purpose, to awaken to our True Selves, our Divine Nature and Divine Inheritance. In this life there is nothing better than this transformation, this connection with Jesus and God. Once you have experienced this Grace you will be eager to return, which you can at any time through meditation. Through your connection with God you will also have many realizations, one truth is that all life is One with God.

There are many ways to go into the quiet to meditate, perhaps you will imagine that you are walking in soft lush green grass and the sun is shining brightly and colorful songbirds are singing and flying around, you smell the fragrant scent of sweet flowers in bloom. A clear running stream is nearby and you hear the sound of a waterfall gently flowing, this is so relaxing you decide to sit down next to this big beautiful shade tree. Now you are relaxed and ready.

Okay, so what are you waiting for? It is time beloveds, turn off the electronics, the TV, stereo, cell phones, your computer anything that will distract you from your true purpose and that is discovering who you truly are. LOVE and JOY, awaken to your Divine Self, claim your Divine Birthright, you are worthy. Oh, there are so many toys to distract us from discovering our true Selves, of course they are very sophisticated technologies, but a distraction all the same. For when we awaken to who we really are we are Free. Forever Free. We no longer need to be slaves to the system. No longer will you be searching for the happiness and love you long for, because you will find the greatest Love is within You. Once you make this connection the synchronicity that transforms your life from the mundane to the miraculous. Every area of your life will improve once you make the connection.

I know what your thinking. How can I find quiet time, I barely have a moment to catch my breath? It is important for your personal well being and health to allow at least 15 - 30 minutes of quiet solitude once a day, twice is even better. You owe it to your Self to enter the silence. You will be so happy you did.

In today's busy world, we can easily get lost in the never ending list of daily activities. "Well, I have to do this and I have to do that" and before we know it the day is over, and another day, and another day. Days turn into weeks, months, years go by, your life goes by. We get caught up in cycles of doing so many things, but many of them do not bring us the joy or happiness we seek. Connecting with your Higher Self will. Everyday we all have at some point a break time, and if you do not have any relax time you most definitely need to create this space for your own inner peace.

It is important to make time for yourself and your Higher Self, to breath and reflect on what is really important in our lives. To evaluate and reassess one's life and take time to slow down and allow your Higher Self to recharge your batteries. To restore your soul in complete silence. Remember we call the shots here. Sometimes we forget that. A very thoughtful person once said to me, "Kimberly, only you takes care of you." When we push ourselves too much and do not restore ourselves then we run our batteries too low. It is important to recharge ourselves, our vital Life Force Energy and how we do this is allowing time for relaxation, meditation, prayer and solitude. Go sit somewhere in nature, by a stream, on a hilltop, a walk in the woods, hear the birds singing to you, feel the sunlight dancing on your face, sit on the beach and hear the waves and watch the sun dancing on the water. Lay in a hammock and watch the white billowing clouds floating by in a blue sky or watch the leaves dancing in the wind. Gaia gives us so many blessings of beauty everywhere we turn.

When you make your connection with your Higher Self, it is absolutely the best feelings of Love you shall ever experience. Until you have connected with your Divine Self there is no other feeling like it in the World. Take all the Love you have ever felt in your entire existence and then multiply that millions of times over, it is just The Most wonderful Love flooding your entire being and world. Believe me you will want to meditate a great deal more to return to the Oneness. The Love and Bliss you will experience is beyond what anyone can ever try to describe in any language. You just have to experience this for yourself. You will be so happy you did. As I said before "Heaven has a language all its own, it is Divine Love." Love is the language you knew before you came here, now is the time to Awaken to your Love Life. Love is where you came from, Love is who you are, Love is where you will return, let this lifestream be the best Love Life by opening your heart to the real You. Here are some meditations to get you started. Relax, breathe and open your heart. I AM OPEN, OPEN, OPEN TO LOVE.

The Heart Meditation

Close your eyes and take three deep cleansing breaths. Your entire body is completely relaxed. Visualize golden white light pouring from your heart center and filling up your entire body full to overflowing surrounding you in an orb of golden white light. You are a shining bright light and the light from your heart center is filling your room with golden white light. You are the light.

Now move your consciousness from your mind to your heart center. You feel yourself moving down into your heart center like floating down the river on a summer day. You feel so good, life is great. You are the beautiful golden white light shining as you move completely into your heart center. Breathe in Light Breathe out Love. Keep breathing and feeling the Divine Love that is emanating from your heart.

Feel the peacefulness and Love that is you. If you see someone ask who they are. You could see Jesus, your angels guides, Archangels, Ascended Masters, family that have passed over. Everyone is different, so each experience will be unique. Isn't that great! Enjoy this wonderful blissful state. As you keep meditating you will feel like you are floating. This is a good thing, keep floating. Stay here for as long as you wish. Come back here often. Namaste.

Chapter Seven

ASKING FOR A SIGN

Have you ever thought about asking for a sign from God? Of course you have, we all have. Did you wait for the answer?

When asking for a sign you can even specify what sign you wish to see. For example: "God if you are there and listening to me then show me a sign. Let me find a penny within the next 24 hours, or a feather, see a rainbow, a bluebird, a butterfly, a dragonfly or angels." You can request any sign you choose. You may be walking along a city street when suddenly you see the very thing you requested, or hear someone talking about it on the radio or see it on a bulletin board, in the news paper, a complete stranger may walk by and just as they pass by you they turn to you and say God's message right to you and only you know the true meaning of the message. You can ask God anything at any time. I prefer a quiet place, but anywhere is the right place if it feels right to you. Whatever you wish to say to God, He is always listening. If your day is so busy that the only place you can find a quiet moment is the bathroom, that is okay also. Do not concern yourself with where you are when you talk to Him, just talk to Him. I personally find I am better at listening in a quiet atmosphere. Your asked for sign can come an any form. If you ask to see a bluebird, you might see a picture of one somewhere, or hear a song with the word bluebird in it. There are many different ways your sign will appear, God is very creative I love that about Him. One way or another you will hear from God.

Did you know that right now you have angels all around you? Yes, you do. They are ready and willing to help you any way they can, but you must first ask for their assistance before they can help you. This is the wonderful gift of Free Will that God gave to each of us. So what are you waiting for, send out your invitation now, because everyone is a MVS (most valuable soul) on God's team. I love finding signs from God especially when I did not ask for a sign because I know God and His angels are all around me guiding me every step of the way. What wonderful conformations when God sends me a sign to tell me "I Love you" or "Give any worries to the angels and know that all is well," and so it is. I love seeing signs of angels around me, especially when I have not asked for a sign. I will see a quick flash of a colored orb and depending on the color I know which Archangels are saying hello. I am thrilled to see the Archangels and Ascended Masters and I thank them for being a part of my daily life. Thank you.

Invite the Heavenly Hosts into your life. I love to invite the Archangels and Ascended Masters into my home. I open the door wide and say, "I invite the Archangels and Ascended Masters into my home, welcome, welcome!" You can also invite the angels to dine with you by putting an extra place setting at the table. Invite the angels and ascended masters into your life daily. They are most eager to hear from us and to help us on our journey.

Chapter Eight

THE VIOLET FLAME

Our lifestreams are on a spiritual path for the soul's evolution on earth is self-mastery, balance our karma then we can return home to the higher realms and dimension. We are all protected by God and our bodies are completely filled and surrounded by His White Light called the Tube of Light and the Self-Luminous Substance of the Mighty Violet Consuming Flame. Calling upon this high-frequency energy of the Violet Flame to blaze through our four lower bodies will help assist us in reaching our goals more quickly.

The Violet Flame transmutes all lower negative energy to higher Divine vibrational frequencies which helps us prepare for our Ascension. The Violet Flame destroys and annihilates everything undesirable, all third dimensional negative feelings, actions, karma, in the cells of our body, purifying our bloodstream, and clearing and illuminating our entire consciousness to be the perfect expression of the Mighty I AM Presence in action. The Violet Flame is a sacred gift from God that completely clears away all karmic debt from this lifestream and all other lifestreams past, present and future. This truly is a magnificent gift from God. For this reason I wish to include a Violet Flame decree so everyone reading this book will be able to transmute all negative energies and karma past, present and future on all levels of existence. The Ascended Masters have used the Violet Consuming Flame to dissolve all discordant creations of their past lives to become the Ascending Masters of Perfection they are today.

VIOLET FLAME DECREES
(repeat each one three times)

I AM the Violet Transmuting Flame cleansing all impure and unnecessary substance from my four lower bodies..

I AM filled from head to toe with the Violet Consuming Flame. Rushing from beneath my feet to above my head my entire being is consumed in the Mighty Whirlwind of The Violet Consuming Flame. I AM restored to perfection of my Mighty I AM Presence in action.

I AM the radiant intensity pressure of the Violet Consuming Flame filling my four lower bodies full to overflowing and clearing and cleansing every cell, atom and electron in my physical body and illuminating my entire consciousness, being and world.

I AM a radiant being of the Violet Consuming Flame blazing through me and consuming and annihilating everything undesirable and imperfect throughout my being and world past, present and future.

While saying these Violet Flame decrees envision the Violet Flame filling your entire body and surrounding you in a large whirlwind flame cleansing your entire being of all impure and unnecessary substance from your four lower bodies. Clearing and cleansing every cell, atom and electron in your body.

There are unlimited ways to do the Violet Flame ceremony, but here is a basic outline. You can modify this any way you choose, just remember it is more important what you feel in your heart, than being absolutely perfect in your ceremony. Speak the words out loud because the words are a positive vibration and the sound makes this sacred ceremony more effective. Imagine a large ball of Violet Fire above your head, now ask the Violet Fire to enter your body and fill every cell and atom of your body, extend the Fire beneath your feet and above your head until the flame completely encircles you inside and out. You are now in a giant pillar of the Violet Flame. Ask the Flame to blaze through you now the Consuming Flame of Divine Love and Compassion. Take all my human self concerns, habits and desires and everything unworthy of Thy Purity out of me and annihilate them cause, effect, record and anything standing in the way of my Ascension, any memory past, present and future. Envision the Violet Flame whirling around your entire body inside and out, you are completely engulfed by the Violet Consuming Flame. The Violet Flame has now transmuted all negative energies and replaced them all with the Divine Golden White Light of Purity of the Mighty I Am Presence.

The Light of God never fails and The Mighty I AM Presence is that Light. AMEN

Where we start
and where we end.
The cloth of time
we weave and mend.

Chapter Nine

DISCOVERING OF SELF — PART 2

How would you like to see all the information about you that has been recorded throughout your history? You can open many doors to the Higher Realms including accessing your Akashic Records also known as The Book of Life. Every thought, word and deed you have ever had, including everything you have learned in all of your lifetimes and you can bring that information into this life. Everything you have ever learned will be revealed to you. Nothing is ever lost that cannot be found, once you remember your gifts you bring that knowledge into this life.

When you discover Self, you suddenly realize this is what you have been looking for all your life. You realize you are a super hero with super powers. To connect with your Higher Self, your God Self is the most wonderful feeling you will experience. The Love, Bliss, Joy, Light, Ecstasy and Grace that one feels all at once, this is Nirvana. You will discover just how absolutely fantastic your Love Life is meant to be. From the core of your existence you will be completely lifted up to Higher levels of consciousness and from this vantage point one can see their life so much more clearly. You will now view your life in a whole new refreshing way. How beautiful we all are, Divine Beings of Love shining brightly. I love the Divine Light that shines in everyone. You are magnificent Angels of Light filled with Divine Love. One day soon, you will awaken to your Divine Benevolence and see yourself as God and all the Heavens see you. You are Love.

When you walk through the door of Light immediately you feel the greatest Love, Happiness, Bliss and Joy, the beautiful Light shining like the Sun filling every space. "Nirvana" is the state of perfect bliss in Buddhism, in which the self is freed from suffering and desire and is united with the Creator of the universe.

TRUTH
Midst darkness
I find my destiny.
For the brightest Light
shines within me.

There are many things to keep us busy, to distract us from doing the one thing that is the most important. To connect with God, to quiet the mind and go deep into our heart center. All of our little electronic gadgets are wonderful, but everything in moderation. We should be present in the now. God wishes for us to socialize more, connect with each other in a positive way. Synchronicity of life, we never know what lies in store for us. What miracle could be waiting just around the next corner. Whatever our plans may be, God takes our dreams and transforms them far beyond our expectations.

Love life

So put away your phones and ear pods, tune in to what is going on around you. Get outside and go for a walk or a ride on your bike. Smile and be happy you are here and life is absolutely fantastic. Be excited and expect wonderful things to manifest right before your eyes, right now. Miracles are unfolding every minute, there is no time like the present enjoy it, our cup overflows with Joy, Love, Bliss and Prosperity. All of life is Sacred, this is why nature heals and restores us.

In meditation, entering the silence we are better able to discover our true nature, gifts and qualities about ourselves we might not have known before. With our new Self knowledge we are able to follow our dreams. When we discover our Life Purpose and follow that path, work is no longer work but a joy. We are thrilled to wake up in the morning and get busy on whatever that purpose may be. As we know from the Law of Attraction the happier we are the higher our vibration is the more we draw things to be happy about. So more great things keep coming into your life. What a wonderful circle of Joy, Happiness, Prosperity and of course Love.

If each person looks within themselves and masters their world (the four lower bodies: mental, emotional, physical, and spiritual), and does not worry about or pass judgement on what anyone else is doing, only concern oneself with mastering who you are then one by one the world will transform into a world of ascended masters. As above so below and so it is.

THE GUIDE
Open your heart
and unlock your mind.
The Light in your soul
is the Loving kind.

When we listen with our hearts and not our mind, we are tuning into our Higher Self, our Christ Consciousness. As we follow the direction our heart points us in then we are being true to ourselves. Honestly you could not have a better source of information than from God. The answers to all your questions lie within yourself. I have always heard that, but it wasn't until I took the journey inward that I could know the Truth. We are magnificent beings of Pure Light Substance (Energy) and our bodies are the temple that house our Divine Souls. Enter the quiet through meditation, discover your True Self and feel God's Love for you. There is nothing else like it in all the World.

Chariot to the Exalted Throne-

Above the sea, a white bird flew by.

While on a souls journey my sister Jenny and I.

Holding hands we dove into a sea of ebony black.

On a spiritual quest there is no turning back.

Our guiding Angel appeared as a small white light.

We followed in Faith all through the night.

Love life

From time to time we would stop and rest.

Travels are far when seeking a vision quest.

A sea of life swimming our way.

Visions like these are not everyday.

Fish of all sizes, colors even stripes.

So many varieties, so many types.

In the distance we saw a white moving pole.

Hovering over it became a white spiral hole.

So down we went as fast as we could swim.

Not to lose our Angel's light that suddenly seemed dim.

Spinning around corners upside down and more.

Reeling we reach the Light....

Heaven's Door.

Standing in the Light who else could it be?

A beautiful winged angel, my grandmother Meme.

"Hurry!" she said, "there's not much time."

Stepping blindly through the Light into Heaven Divine.

Looking around in amazement at what I was seeing,

A place filled with angels and Heavenly beings.

A formal engagement of white robes and full wings.

Words are lost, unable to describe such sacred things.

Heaven has a language all its own.
A sense of Knowing without being told.
A party of Angels. One Higher than the rest.
With a Mer-ka-bah holding the Sun upon His chest.
Raising eyes only, honored in His Grace.
Feeling the Oneness, the Love in His place.
Blind faith opened my eyes to see.
The true beauty of Eternity.

When God answers your prayers, questions or wishes the answers are always so simple and so profound at the same time. I love the way God teaches with such love, compassion and tenderness. There have been times when things occurred in my life and I could not understand why these things were happening. It wasn't until later that I realized why something occurred when it did, everything unfolds in Divine Order. Source was closing one door while another door was opening, creating my dreams come true. I am so much happier with my expanded view, an idea comes to me and I say "Aaaahhh NOW I see, NOW I understand why my life unfolded the way it did. Source was leading me here, the steps I was taking were literally answers to my prayers.

I have always talked to God, but it wasn't until I was in my early twenties that I noticed God answering me. I am sure He always has answered me throughout my life, I was just not tuned in and listening. This particular day I was having one of those moments where I was feeling so alone. I was longing for that special man to come into my life, real love, joy and happiness. In my despair I wrote a poem I named "Our Prelude" and in the poem I am asking "is anyone out there, or am I all alone here? Can you find me? Is all communication dead?" While I was writing this poem guess what? God joined the conversation. He told me that I am not alone. I said I was sinking and He said, "Quick, grab My hand. Let Us start slowly Our Prelude." I now understand that God talks to us all the time. The question we have to ask ourselves, "Are we listening to the answers God is giving us to the questions that we put before Him?"

Our Prelude

Here I await for the leaving of this sad, dreary place in my heart. To colorful, joyful times, sweet dew drops moisten my lips like a kiss. I know you will be coming soon to take me home.

Dark!! Yes, somber dark here. The sunshine lies dormant in my heart waiting for you to come and unlock my soul. Laughter can be heard in the rafters of my memories, lost once again in the shadows. Can you find me? Are all communications dead? PLEASE, try again! I am still here anticipating your arrival. You must not let me down, for I am already sinking.

Quick!! Grab My hand! Hold on tightly! Let Us start slowly, Our Prelude. The music shall come with no effort. For Our Love will free each movement to perfection. As the scores play on, each note will bring Us eternal light to Our souls. So play on my dear. For I have waited long for Our Song.

Chapter Ten

MUSIC

THE LANGUAGE OF LOVE

**E'tude -
Ask of Love many a thing. All Love asks is that you sing.**

Throughout my life, there have been many expressions from God that our life is a composition of music that We are co-creating together. Everything in the Universe is vibration, our lives are music playing in the Etheric Realms. We are God's musical instruments and our songs (our lives) we play are part of Heaven's orchestra to co-create the Music of Life. We are the songwriters, creating the songs of Life with God. We need to start asking ourselves "What kind of music are we creating?" "Happy Love songs, God I hope so."

Everything in the Universe is vibration and while there are different variations, high or low we are all Love's Divine vibrational energy.

Music is a great healer. There is so much more to music that we have yet to discover. These are very exciting times we live in now, miracles are occurring everywhere. Gifts from Heaven "praise be to God." Often times we hear a song that resonates with our entire being. Everything about the song is just perfect. It does not matter where we are, when we hear the music we get so excited "that's the song, that's my song, turn it up please." We immediately feel great just listening to music. For example; one moment your driving down the road it is an average day when all the sudden you favorite song is playing on the radio, now you are singing and moving to the music feeling fantastic. Your vibration has just soared through the roof literally. See how easy it is. Music resonates with our beings, sometimes we want to jump up and dance, to move to the music in whatever creative way we feel. Music is liberating and it can dissolve all negative energies from our past in an instant. We are happy, we are filled with joy. We know that when we play classical music for our plants and flowers they flourish. One of the quickest ways to raise our vibration is to play one of our favorite songs. Now you are in alignment with God, and now you are creating wonderful things in your life. Wow, just that quick and easy that really is a miracle.

Overture -
To hear your sweet voice
pours gold through gray.
Given a choice
with You I will stay.
A love unknown
to man or beast.
To hold us together when
Our odds seem the least.

Love life

**When you are ready, come to Me.
Together we will set
Our love free.**

Chapter Eleven

THE POWER OF LOVE

THE KEY -
Dancing in Heaven while the angels sing,
Love is the key, Kimberly,
Dancing in Heaven while the angels sing,
Love is the key to everything.

<u>Oneness</u>
Give unselfishly and so be given.
Love in abundance and so be loved.

Love is the most powerful energy throughout all the Universes. Love is all there is, the rest is illusion, fear is just an illusion there is only Love. What ever your fears may be give them to Love, to God, and forget it because it is done. God takes care of everything for us if we just allow Him to. Everything is possible through Love. EVERYTHING! Everything is created from Love. We are made from Love in Love's image, so this means we are very powerful also. Anything you desire Love will manifest for you, it is a gift from Love that we all possess. You may ask how do I manifest my dearest wishes, how do I make my dreams come true? Through your intent. Creative visualization, the Law of Attraction it really is that simple.

Love life

Love creates worlds, stars, universes. Love has infinite possibilities and so do you, because you are created from Love and you are a loving creator. The moment you realize and take responsibility for your thoughts and actions, your entire life will start to change for the better, because you will change the way you look and think about the world and yourself and everything in it. The realization that you are in control of your life and destiny is the first step, take responsibility, now envision your life the way you would Love for it to be. Imagine all the wonderful happy details and manifest your Love Life. Now is the time to remember who you are so that you will become a conscious creator, what you believe you create. What is belief? Belief is the marriage of thought and emotion. If you believe something to be true you will create it. If you believe you are successful, even if at this moment you are not, you will be successful, also if you believe you will never be successful then that is what you will be. It is all up to you and what you believe. There is nothing or no one that can hold you back but yourself. Everything you have created in your life you believed you could achieve it and so you did. The same goes for what you believe you could not achieve. The fact is, what you did not achieve you could have if you had just believed in yourself. There is nothing that you cannot be, do or have. All things are possible. Jesus taught us that long ago. Everything IS possible. You are Love and this is your Life. A life filled with infinite Love possibilities. A Life you can Love. A Love Life. A life to Love and be Loved.

Love has no boundaries, no limits and it can move you through space and time. This is who you truly are LOVE, LOVE, LOVE, my beloveds, so do not waste another precious now moment on anything else but LOVE. Now you know and now you are on the most important journey Love yourself and others unconditionally. The most important time is and always will be NOW. Now Forgiveness, Now Peace, Now Joy, Now Bliss, Now Love!

Everything in the Universe is vibration. It is important that everyday we work on raising our vibratory levels higher and you can ask the ascended masters and archangels and your personal angel guides to help you do this. The ascended masters, archangels, our angel guides and our I AM Presence (our Higher Selves) vibrates at very high levels and in order for us to hear them or see them we must raise our vibratory level while they are lowering theirs to communicate with us. It is much easier for us to raise our vibratory level than it is for the higher realms to lower theirs. Reach for the Heavens. There are many ways in which we can raise our vibration. One of the best ways is to allow more Love into your life. You can achieve this by radiating more love from yourself through meditation, spending time outside in nature, eating healthy foods like raw fruits, nuts and vegetables, detoxing the body of chemicals, smiling, and singing.

Chapter Twelve

FORGIVENESS

Forgiveness -
The Light of forgiveness
may your heart instill.
This is Heaven's Will.
Once I forgive everyone else,
I can finally see clear
to forgive myself.

The principle of forgiveness I learned many years ago. As a child I was taught "To err is human, to forgive is Divine." God forgives us everyday so why don't we forgive others and ourselves from the slights to the heartbreaking incidents that happen in our lives? Why, you may ask, because our ego stands in the way, coaxing and tormenting us by saying that we have been offended, hurt or insulted in some way. When you hear that voice in your mind say, "You should not allow them to do this or that to you," or "you had better do something about that because you can't let them get away with that." This is where your heart (God) will step in and say, "let it go, walk away, it's not worth it, forget about it." Listen to your heart, you can do this, you always have a choice and if you do just walk away from the curse, you will be the better for it. This is when we let it go, let this pass through you like a warm summer breeze. Do not except that negativity as your reality.

Years ago I learned to "Be a mirror and reflect." Which is saying that if you do not allow the negativity or curse that someone sends to you to affect you, do not speak about it to anyone, the negative energy that was sent to you will bounce off of you "like a mirror and reflect back" and go right back to the sender. Do not except the curses of others and do not send any out. Now that we have moved into the higher dimensions everything we do automatically comes back to us TEN FOLD. So it is for your best interest to only send loving vibrations out to others and yourself. Send blessings out to everyone. You do not have to be friends with them, just don't be an enemy either. I say, "God bless you and your family," and I move on.

As you would not send negative energy out to others do not direct any at yourself either. When you dislike anything about your self you are cursing yourself. When we pass judgments, either about ourselves or others that is a curse of negative energy. No more of that please, for your own good and the highest good of all.

All of my life I have been good at forgiving people. I did not wish to stay mad at anyone because it just did not feel right to me. It did not resonate with my soul being. Anger, resentment, jealously, disappointment, doubt, worry, blame, revenge, hatred, rage, insecurity, guilt, unworthiness, fear, grief, despair, powerlessness are all negative energy and you know this by your emotions. Negative emotions causes a dis-ease in the body and if they are not transmuted and replaced by positive energy, the negativity will eventually manifest itself as disease in the physical body. Yes, you can transmute these lower emotions to higher levels of positive energies. You are a very powerful Divine creator and holding onto negative emotions will literally make you sick.

One of the biggest lessons I learned was that I really was very unforgiving with myself. If I ever made a mistake in any way, oh boy, was I in big trouble with me. Then one day I realized that I could forgive others, but when it came to myself, I was most unforgiving for anything I thought I may have done. How could I ever do that! I really would mentally crucify myself. Other people can make mistakes, but no, not me. I was not allowed to make mistakes, ever. Forgiveness of self was a transforming realization. If I thought I said something that hurt someone's feelings, that just crushed my heart. I would never intensionally hurt another person. If I did anything that I thought I should not have, I would mentally beat myself up for days, or longer, analyzing the situation, replaying the events in my mind like a bad movie that never seems to end. Here was one of my biggest mistakes, I would keep replaying the situation in my mind, thus creating more of the same things that I did not want in my life. When we do things we wish we haven't just say from your heart, "I'm sorry, please forgive me" and move on learning from the lesson so we do not repeat it in the future. As it turns out, later I would find out that when I thought I had been rude to someone, they thought nothing of it. The issues that needed to be dealt with were all within myself, that is why I felt bad, because I needed to cleanse myself.

Here is where we can stop the negative train of events that keep coming around in our lives. One day, this thought came to me, "If I could forgive others for things they did, why can't I do the same for me?" Sounds so simple and it really is, but I put myself through a great deal of mental torment for many years, before I had this one simple realization. That is when I was inspired to write my poem on Forgiveness.

Forgiveness is one the most important things we do for ourselves. When we forgive others, for what ever reason, we are not so much letting them off the hook as we are freeing ourselves from the negative toxic energy that accompanies these feelings. Someone could hurt us once, or we might hurt someone, but we in turn hurt ourselves hundreds of times, every time we relive the story in our minds we are nailing ourselves to the cross. This is why it is a great idea to forgive and forget. Do yourself a favor and let it go. Live and let live.

As I said before, when we hold onto negative feelings about ourselves or others we are only hurting ourselves. If you send out negative feelings to someone, this negative energy will only come back to you TEN FOLD. Remember the Law of Attraction I spoke of earlier. Like attracts like. So yes, it is best to let go of any negative feelings past or present. Let them go and free yourself from the weight of this unwanted toxic baggage you have been carrying around, you will see what a great weight has now been lifted from your shoulders. Breathe in three long deep cleansing breaths. With each breath you are releasing all fears, doubts, jealousy, hatred and you are replacing them with joy, love, happiness, bliss and compassion. Let go of all that old baggage and feel yourself lifting up to higher vibrational levels. How wonderful this new positive energy feels so light and free. If need be ask God for forgiveness (ask and it is always given) and now forgive yourself. I think you will discover as I did what an uplifting feeling one gets by releasing yourself from this enslaving negative energy. Live a much happier life everyday. Let go of the negative baggage, don't carry the guilt trips with you. Gladly, leave them behind forever.

I know what you are thinking, "how... how can I after all that has happened to me, how can I just let it go?" You are a Magnificent Divine child of God and you can do anything you wish to do and the sooner you let go of unhealthy negative feelings the faster your life is going to turn around into the direction you wish it to go. To become the person you wish to be you must forgive others and then forgive yourself for all the wrongs you believe you have done or has been done to you in your lifetime. Start a fresh new clean chapter in your life, don't bring yesterdays garbage with you, throw it away. When you move into a new home, you don't bring the garbage with you, you leave it behind in the dumpster. Time for closure of the old chapter and start a new life, a new story and you are the star on your new wonderful adventure. You can be whoever you wish to be, remember you are a super hero with super powers. What are you passionate about?

How do I get started, you may ask? This is an important step for each of us to take to release old patterns that keep coming back around in our lives. Write down on a piece of paper the names of all the people that you feel wronged you in some way, now say, "I forgive you" and release your feelings to Heaven and know that Heaven is healing this situation in all ways. See the person or persons involved and surround them in a big pink bubble and release them to Heaven. See the pink bubble floating up into the Heavenly Realms. God will take care of everything. Now ask for forgiveness from all the people you have wronged in some way in your lifetime and forgive yourself and feel the healing from Heaven. Do you feel a great weight has been lifted from your shoulders? You are also releasing old karma, let it go, negative emotions do not serve anyone. The pink bubble works for all situations you would like Heaven's help with.

By letting go you free yourself from the toxic waste caused by the negative energy and you will feel better in many ways. Through this releasing you can awaken to all new possibilities. Because you are closing the door to an old way of thinking and living and opening the door to a new positive ways of experiencing life, thus creating

Love life

more loving, happy life choices, new doors will open that you did not realize existed.

Chapter Thirteen

MAGNIFICENT BELOVED ANGELS

So magnificent angels are you envisioning your magnificent Love life, Divine purpose, ideal life style, your own successful business, new inventions that will revolutionize the way we live on Mother Gaia, great health and well being and the greatest happiness you can imagine? Once you decide what it is you truly wish to experience, keep those thoughts in your mind and heart and think of nothing else but your intended outcome. Do not worry yourself with the how to's, leave that to Heaven, only concentrate on the most positive manifestations. Then pay attention to the ideas that come to you, write them down. Follow your intuition and the dreams and visions you receive. Envision yourself in the reality you wish to thrive in. Remind yourself often that everything is possible. EVERYTHING! Trust, Trust, Trust! Know without a shadow of doubt that Heaven is bringing you all that you desire and so it is.

Know that what we consider to be mistakes are in reality tools to help us realize what we truly wish to have in our lives. There are no mistakes, just stepping stones down the path of our most magnificent journey. We try things on in life and some things fit us perfectly, while other things do not. So we keep looking for what fits us best now. The things that worked perfectly for us last week, may not work this week. Know this is part of our journey, to try new things all the time. Don't be afraid to follow your hearts desire, confidently walk through the new doors that are opening to you now, follow your dreams, whatever they may be. How boring life would be to do the very same thing all the time especially if it does not resonate with our soul and make our heart sing. This is the blessings of change, sometimes we have to be gently nudged along and sometimes we need a major kick in the bottom to get us to change our direction that puts us on our Divine life path. Try something new, look at the world with new eyes, the eyes of children look at the world in wonder and excitement. Children haven't been conditioned yet, remove the veil of old conditioning and look with the eyes of a child. Children make friends easily, they follow their instincts and love unconditionally. You remember that, you were a child once. When we change our perspective and view the world with more love, our lives change for the better. The world changes for the better one person at a time. Your positive loving energies also attract more positive loving experiences in your life. The wonderful infinity flow of Love.

Once you are in alignment with your Self, your entire life falls into place, life flows so easily, you feel like you are on top of the world. Love is who we are, where we came from and where we all shall return. Love is all there is and either you are allowing the flow of Love into your life or you are blocking the flow of Love with your negative thoughts, feelings and vibrations. Once those blocks are removed Love flows to you freely and effortlessly. Love yourself for all that your are because you are most worthy beloveds. You are God Individualized and God made you perfect just the way you are. You carry all the information of the Universe within you. You are like the most sophisticated computer and your programs are completely loaded and ready to run. You have much more than just a Life 101 handbook, you have all the Universal libraries within you. You are Divine Intelligence.

Be happy and love yourself, believe in yourself. Put your hand on your heart center and say three times "I Love (your full name)." Where ever you go, share your love with everyone you meet by giving them your smile. Smiles are free to give but priceless to receive. Love and compassion is the best investment one can make, these are the most valuable shares and yet they are free, and the dividends pay ten fold. Image Love coming back to you ten times more powerful from all the Love you express. A continuous infinity flow of Love that grows more powerful every minute. All that Love adds up to a blissfully happy and fulfilled Love Life. How magnificent you are. You are Divine Love.

INDIVISIBLE -
Love for all!
For all are One.
Guided by our Father Sun.

A CLEAR VIEW -
Clear the view,
Love gazes at me.
Breathless....
You are all I see.

A Clear View I wrote after meeting Jesus in meditation. All of my writings are inspired from connecting with Jesus and my I AM Presence.

Love Life every minute. Many blessings of Love.
And so it is.   Namaste'

www.ingramcontent.com/pod-product-compliance
Lightning Source LLC
Chambersburg PA
CBHW020017050426
42450CB00005B/519